Becoming a Man, Son, King and Priest Today

WILLIE G. MILLER JR

WILLIE G. MILLER JR.

© **Copyright 2025 by Willie Glen Miller Jr.**

All rights reserved. No part of this book may be photocopied or reproduced in any form without written permission from the publisher. Moreover, no part of this publication can be stored in a retrieval system, transmitted by any means, recorded, or otherwise copied, without written permission from the author or the publisher.

Legal Notice

This book is copyright protected. This book is only for personal use. You cannot amend, distribute, sell, use, quote or paraphrase any part or the content within this book, without the consent of the author or publisher.

Limits of Liability and Disclaimer of Warranty

Please note the information contained within this document is for educational purposes only. All effort has been made to present accurate, up to date, and reliable, complete information. No warrantees of any kind are declared or implied. Readers acknowledge that the author is not engaging in the rendering of legal, financial, medical, or professional advice. The contents within this book have been derived from various sources.

By reading this document, the reader agrees that under no circumstances is the author responsible for any losses, direct, or indirect, which are incurred because of the use of the information contained within this document, including, but not limited to, errors, omissions, or inaccuracies.

BECOMING A MAN, SON, KING & PREIST TODAY!

TABLE OF CONTENTS

APPRECIATION 4

DEDICATION 5

PREFACE 6

INTRODUCTION 8

BECOMING A MAN 10

HOW AND WHERE TO THINK 16

GETTING AN UNDERSTANDING 24

HOW TO SPEAK 32

BECOMING A SON 36

BECOMING A KING 49

BECOMING A PRIEST 67

CONCLUSION 86

ABOUT THE AUTHOR 88

CONNECT AND SHARE 89

REFERENCES 90

APPRECIATION

To Beverley—My Queen and My Fire

Girl, you are proof that when God sends help, He sends excellence. Your love lifts me, your faith fuels me, and your presence brings peace to every room I walk in.

You don't just support the vision—you expand it. You've been my loudest cheerleader, my wisest counsel, and the fire that keeps me focused.

This book? It carries your prayers, your push, and your unshakable belief in who God called me to be.

I love you. I honor you. I thank God for you. We're just getting started—let's keep taking ground together.

Luv, Luv, Luv,

Bill

DEDICATION

To every young man trying to find out who they are and refuse to become another statistic —

To every man who refuses to stay where life left him —

To every son who is daring to believe he's loved and chosen —

To every king who is ready to build what hell cannot tear down —

To every priest who is willing to carry God's presence into a broken world —

This is for you!

May you rise!

May you reign!

May you BECOME!

PREFACE

This book was born out of burden and fire. For too long, too many men (young and old) have been left wandering — gifted by God, but unsure of who they are. Present in life but absent in purpose. I've seen it. I've lived it. I know the battle.

The truth is: no man becomes who he's called to be by accident. You do not just wake up one day fully formed. Becoming a man, a son of God, a king, and a priest requires intentional pursuit. It demands surrender. It demands transformation. It demands a decision. This journey isn't about checking religious boxes or living for applause. It's about answering the call to rise — to become who God always intended you to be.

In these pages, I am not giving you a formula. I am not offering you shallow motivation or a blueprint for world success. I am handing you a mirror. I am placing a sword in your hand. I am calling you to become. Every chapter is designed to walk you deeper into identity, authority, and intimacy with God — not so you can wear a title, but so you can live as a true son, reign as a faithful king, and serve as a bold priest in a world that desperately needs men of God to stand up and lead.

This is not just a personal journey. It is a generational one. The choices you make to become will echo far beyond your lifetime. I pray that as you read these words, you will not just be inspired. You will be ignited.

BECOMING A MAN, SON, KING & PREIST TODAY!

The time for passive manhood is over. The world is waiting. Heaven is watching. And our Father is calling.

Let us answer Him — together.

INTRODUCTION

This is not a book for the passive man. This is not a book for the men who are content with sitting on the sidelines and never understanding their one destiny. This is a call — a summons — for every man who knows deep down that he was born for more. This book is about awakening you to understand that you were born for a Kingdom. You were born to conquer this battlefield called life. You were born for a crown.

But before you can take your God given place, you must *become!*

- **Become a Man** — one forged in the fires of discipline, faith, and truth. A man whose strength comes not from pride, but from the Spirit of God dwelling within him.

- **Become a Son** — a man who knows he belongs. A son who carries the Father's authority because he carries the Father's heart.

- **Become a King** — entrusted to take territory, to steward resources, to defend what is righteous, and to establish the Kingdom wherever God sends him.

- **Become a Priest** — one who kneels before he conquers, who ministers in the secret place before he moves in public strength.

This becoming will not happen by comfort.

It will not happen by chance.

It will take a fight — the right fight — against every lie, every fear, every limitation that tried to hold you back.

The road to manhood, sonship, kingship, and priesthood is costly. It will cost you your excuses. It will cost you your comfort. It will cost you your old way of living and thinking. But what you gain will be worth everything:

- Your identity.
- Your authority.
- Your territory.
- Your legacy.

This world does not just need more men. It needs more sons, more kings, more priests — who know who they are and who are not afraid to walk in it.

This is the becoming.

This is the call.

The only question left is — will you answer?

Let's go!

CHAPTER 1

BECOMING A MAN

"When I was a child, I spoke as a child, I understood as a child, I thought as a child: but when I became a man, I put away childish things."
— 1 Corinthians 13:11

Every young boy long for the day when they will become a man. In fact, as men, we refer to one another with terms that support the idea that we are men. For example, "You Da Man", What's up BOSS, and how about - all right CHAMP! These terms suggest that we view ourselves and other men properly or as equals. Topically this is based solely on our perception of one another's social and economic status. If we look the part or dress the part, we are held in higher esteem than others which suggest to them we are grown men. This, however, is troubling because how we look or carry ourselves in one instance is not a determining factor of weather, we are men or not. Even more troubling is, in the United States, parents, school systems and churches have failed our young men by not defining a clear transition point from childhood into manhood and a curriculum of sort to prepare them for the transition.

In the United States, the defining moment of transitioning into manhood is not identifiable. We are told we become adults when we turn eighteen years old however, it is not clear when we become men. Yes, turning eighteen years old in the United States gives you rights as an adult to make your own decisions, but it also provides that right to be punished as an adult if those decisions lead to criminal activity. Additionally, I question, if I become a man at the age of eighteen, why can't I have an alcoholic drink until I am 21 years old? This question supports the fact, our transition into manhood is not clear in the United States as it is in other cultures.

Some cultures provide their young men with rites of passage. Although some of the ceremonies seem questionable, they serve as a point of transition from a child into manhood. For example, in the Jewish culture, when a boy turns 13 years old, they read from the Torah in front of the congregation followed by a Bar Mitzvah (Hebrew for "Son of the Commandment"). From that date, he is recognized as a man and has rights and obligations of a Jewish male adult. With that, he is expected to participate in synagogue services and take his place in the Jewish community and to demonstrate his manhood.

The Hamar Tribe of southwest Ethiopia has a unique way of initiating boys into manhood, "bull jumping". During the ceremony, as a demonstration of patronage, female relatives dance and invite whipping from the boy who is being introduced into manhood. The scar from whipping gives them a say in who they marry. After dancing and whipping, castrated bulls are placed in a row side to side and the boy runs back and forth across two times. If he fails, he is ridiculed. If successful, he crosses over into manhood.

In the United States, you are considered a man on your 18th birthday. The only indicators of this non-recognized transition are you might need to register for the military draft or as a voter. There are no ceremonies, you really do not know what comes next because no one has taken the time to provide you with any instructions. So, you go to college, enlist in the military, get a job at the mall, get married, have a baby, etc. Not knowing, none of those decisions make you a man.

Dad, when will I know I have become a man? Dad, when do I get to walk in your shoes? These questions ring loud and are hard to respond to. I wish I could tell my son that once you become a 13, 16, 18 or 21-year-old you are a man. That would be great! If at that given moment, you would have all the experience and knowledge that I obtained doing a lifetime of learning. The life lessons that come through making mistakes, falling, and failing, and getting back on my feet again. I only wish it was that simple. Unfortunately, it is NOT!

While practicing ministry, I had the opportunity to serve as the Vice President of the Men's Ministry. One evening we called a meeting with the men to determine what group of teachings would be beneficial for them. That evening men from ages 16 – 50 attended. As leaders, we wanted to focus on developing boys into men and men into men. So, in our search to understand the dynamics of the group, we asked the question. How did you know when you become or became a man? The responses were interesting. One gentleman responded, when I reached my 18th birthday. Another, when I moved out of my mother's house. Another, I became a man on my 30th birthday. Lastly, a gentleman responded when I had my first baby, I became a man. In that moment, it became clear to me in our community and culture, we have not been effective at defining stages in our male children's lives where we have increased expectations for them that lead them to becoming men.

Intrigued by their responses to the question, I decided to ask my 14-year-old son the question. Son, when will you know you have become a man? He responded when I got out of high school and reached my 18th birthday. He was surprised when I said no to both of his responses. With a gentle smile, I proceeded to tell him about a 50+ year old man I met on a fishing boat. This man introduced himself to me and proceeded to boast about his womanizing exploits. He talked about how he was "running these young women" out in these streets. He had no respect for women or himself. Listening closely to this man, I realized he was a mature man from a physical and age perspective however, his behavior was like a child and his lack of discipline and reckless behavior was alarming and disappointing. What I learned in that conversation, this man spoke like a child, had childlike understanding, and his thoughts were childish. He did not understand the implications of his actions and that was followed by his immature conversation so therefore, I explained to my son that we become men when we stop speaking, understanding, and thinking like children.

The scripture declares: "When I was a child, I spoke as a child, I understood as a child, I thought as a child: but when I became a man, I put away childish things" (1 Corinthians 13:11). With that, I told my son with proper grooming and mentoring, he could begin his transition into manhood today. He would be positioned to enter manhood and could be further ahead than men double his age. Yes, I believe he could begin his transition into manhood and become a man quicker than some men who are 30, 40 and even 50-years-old.

The Apostle Paul says when we speak first, without thinking, our lack of understanding shows because we have not taken time to think about what we are saying. When we do this, we are acting childish – silly and immature. This happens with adults because we, like children, do not understand the power of thought and the strength that is displayed in knowing what we are talking about. Steven Covey in his book "7 Habits of Highly Effective People" cautions us to "Seek first to understand and then to be understood". Basically, make sure we know what we are talking about before we open our mouths. If we are going to put away childish things, and transition into manhood, we must change the order of our actions to the following:

1. Thinking
2. Understanding
3. Speaking.

The elements of 1 Corinthians 13:11 are the building blocks for how we should function in life as adults. If we deal with it from an adultlike perspective, the scripture will read like this: I put away childish things. Now I **think** as a man, **understand** as a man, and **speak** as a man (I Corinthians 13:11).

Entering Manhood means we understand the value and importance of thinking and understanding before we speak. *Manhood is really about mentality.* Not just about having a way that we think, but just as important, having the ability to think, learn and articulate what we know to be our truth. So, if we want to be a man, we need to know:

1. **How to think** - the power and place of thoughts.
2. **How to gain understanding** - the power of learning and knowing.
3. **How to speak** - the power and authority in releasing our sound.

CHAPTER 2

HOW AND WHERE TO THINK

"Mind power is one of the strongest and most useful powers you possess."
— Remez Sasson

In the article "Mind Power – The Power of Thoughts", Remez Sasson argues that giving attention to and becoming passionate about our thoughts makes our thoughts powerful enough to affect our reality. It can seem unrealistic because thoughts are invisible. However, as improbable as it may seem, they materialize into our lives in unique ways. For example, Facebook, Snapchat, Microsoft, Lamborghini, Corvette, and the home you live in are all products of someone's thoughts that affected their reality and even more powerful, they also affect ours. All the things I mentioned started as ideas in someone's mind. Reminding us that we cannot underestimate the power of our thoughts because we are products of what we think.

"The Mind is a Terrible Thing to Waste." – The United Negro College Fund. This slogan has become part of our modern-day vernacular and holds as much truth today as it did when it originated over 30 years ago. I agree with it wholeheartedly. The focus was on attracting members of the African American community and to inspire them to enroll in college by providing financial support. However, in a literal sense, it caused me to realize, I must take time to think through things that affect my life and others. I must understand how to think and where to think. You might be thinking, did he say, "Where? Yes, I did! The place of our thoughts within our being is critical. For the bible declares, "As a man thinks in his heart, so is he! (Proverbs 23:7). Once I learned the principle of thinking in my heart, I watched my life transform exponentially.

Grasping this concept is critical, because our ability to think must translate to an understanding that is deep enough in our spirit that we can speak and execute our thoughts. Then and only then can thoughts materialize and be realized into our lives. When I gained the understanding of this principle, I became a man. It all started with understanding that I need to be capable of thinking.

Strangely, the concept of thinking is foreign to many churches and religious institutions around the world. Some spiritual leaders will tell you that learning anything outside of the bible and religious constructs is not for us. This could not be further from the truth because thinking is critical to our success in the world and in the Kingdom of God. Apostle Yolanda Powell expressed this best when she said with conviction, "God needs intelligent people!" People who use their minds to create ideas, form opinions, and make decisions. It is through this creative process that we remain agile and capable of evolving and adapting in an ever-changing world. For without thought, we will never be able to bring the Kingdom of God into the earth, continue to live, prosper, and make our lives successful. By thinking, we move from revelation to revelation, challenge old concepts and models of thought and make them better.

Now that we understand what it means to think, let us explore the importance of where we think. Thoughts that generate within our heads are okay but, to a large degree, we forget those things and they are never manifested in our lives. For thoughts to become a part of our lives, they must transfer from our minds into our hearts. The bible declares, as a man thinks in his heart, so is he (Proverbs 23:7). This scripture is powerful because it shows us that there is an immediate return on whatever energy we invest into thinking when the thoughts reside in our heart. The thoughts we deposit in our hearts are what we are immediately. Just because we do not see it right away and may not have received it materially in our hands, does not mean we have not become it and have it immediately. Please, do not be deceived, we become what we think!

I know, it is hard to conceive of becoming a thing that we think about, and it materializes into the natural realm. Believe it! At times during our walks with God, we will find it hard to believe by faith, we have received what we physically cannot see. Similarly, our faith our belief becomes the substance that what we desire God to do has occurred and will soon materialize from the spiritual realm into the natural realm. The scripture says, "Now faith is the substance of things hoped for, the evidence of things not seen." (Hebrews 11:1). Now! In the context of time, means today, currently, immediately, instantly our faith and belief become the proof or substance that we have what we are believing

God for. It is the same with our heart thoughts but even more powerful.

The Faith Challenge

Having faith and belief in God requires more work on the part of the believer. Once we make a request of God, we still must actively engage ourselves to ensure our belief remains intact while we wait. Sometimes, this is difficult depending on the circumstances surrounding what we are believing God for. For example, believing God for healing from a life-threatening disease verses a new job opportunity when you already have a job has vastly different circumstances. If our faith fails while we are believing God for healing, we could die. If it fails on the new job opportunity, we miss the job and wait for the next opportunity. Maintaining our faith requires more work and the risk of failing is greater than when our thoughts become products of our heart.

With heart-thought, once we place the thought in our heart, our heart will implement it. Once our thoughts become issues of our heart, they are going to flow out of us. When issues flow out of our heart, our body, soul, and spirit respond and cause an alignment both within us and outside of us - the universe. Before we realize it, we are feeling different emotionally, physically, and mentally and without any more thought, things begin to align around us and whatever we need for the thing to materialize comes to us. Resources in the form of people, money, infrastructure, healing, deliverance, inspiration, revelation, etc. come to us.

There is a flow that comes out of our hearts. Our heart releases whatever is placed into them. Solomon admonishes his sons in Proverbs 4:23 to keep their hearts with all diligence, for out of it are the issues of life". King Solomon is saying, "Son carefully maintain your heart because what gets into your heart is what is going to come out. In short if you allow hurt to abide in your heart, hurt is flowing out. Hence the term, hurt people-hurt people. If you allow good feelings of great memories into your heart, good feelings of great memories will flow out of it. So, maintaining and preserving our hearts is a process of ***being aware of and controlling*** what thoughts we allow into our hearts. In a simple sense, we are diligently guarding our heart thoughts! Determining what we allow our hearts to think about because whether good or bad thoughts are who we are or are becoming. Additionally, controlling what we think about in our heart controls what flows out of it. If we learn how to master this, we can issue/supply thoughts into our hearts for distribution for official purposes from our soulish and spiritual realms into the flow of our natural lives (physical realms). Remember, the heart implements whatever thoughts are placed there and we immediately become the thoughts in our heart. As a man thinks in his heart, so is he (Proverbs 23:7).

In Psalm 119:11, King David announces to the Lord, thy word I have hid in my heart that I might not sin against thee. If you are like me, I asked how can we hide words in our blood pumping heart? Well, wed cannot hide anything in your natural blood pumping heart. If we tried, our hearts would stop beating and we would no longer be alive. Later in the text at verse 15 and 16, David declares that he will delight himself in God's statutes and he will not forget His word because he will meditate on them. Looking at this text, it becomes clear, when David is talking about his heart he is talking about his mind because the natural heart is not capable of thought. We can use only our minds to be mindful and to focus on thoughts or activities. We can only train our minds to be attentive and aware. When we do this, our minds become clear and focused, and we become emotionally stable. Because we are thinking in our hearts. Heart-thought brings us into a state of single-mindedness. In this state, we become stable in our conduct, beliefs, and activities. When we are double-minded, we cannot make up our minds and we become unstable in all our ways (James 1:8). Remember, we are constantly becoming what we think. If we allow our thoughts to be all over the place, we will be all over the place. If we are double minded, wavering in our thoughts, undecided and vacillating from one thought to the next, that is what we are and or will be. Our behavior will be unstable; we will not be capable of completely executing on what we think because what we think is a moving target. We become incapable of following one course until we achieve success because the course is constantly changing. Complete success will always elude us. Instability in thought causes instability in everything we are and are constantly becoming!

When I was introduced to this scripture the first time, I was fascinated and thought to myself, King Solomon is on to something. This revelation is hot from the mouth of God into his ear. As I delved deeper, I had the connection to what I believe King

Solomon is referring to when he speaks of thinking in our heart. I believe he is referring to the subconscious mind.

The place of heart thought

The word heart is expressed frequently in the bible. Though the number of times varies depending on the version it still is significant. For example, the word heart appears more than 500 times in the New International Version (NIV) and more than 800 times in the King James Version (KJV). Looking closer, we see the word heart in the Greek means the mind.

In his book "How to Unleash the Power of Your Subconscious Mind", Dr. Joseph Murphy explains the two levels of the mind – the conscious level which deals with rational thought and sub-conscious level which deals with creative and intuitive thoughts. He explains further that there is an exchange of ideas from the conscious mind to the sub-conscious mind. Additionally, once the subconscious mind excepts ideas from the conscious mind, it immediately take action to implement them. This happens with good and bad ideas and without effort from us. ***This is heart thought in action.*** Heart thought draws on everything inside of us without asking for permission to bring whatever we give to life. Solomon was talking about this space – the sub-conscious mind as the heart of man. In plain language, the scripture would read: As a man thinks in his sub-conscious mind, so is he.

It's argued that the subconscious mind controls 85% - 90% of what we do without our awareness. The subconscious mind is powerful and will implement whatever it is given without our approval. If we experience trauma in our lives, if it becomes a condition of our hearts, we will experience the effects of the trauma in our lives because out of our heart flows the issues of life (Proverbs 4:23). In a lot of cases, we are experiencing crazy things in our lives without understanding that we need to be aware of our emotions because they are indicators of the thoughts of the subconscious mind. Training our subconscious mind is not easy but we need to understand the power of our mind and how it frames our character and lives. Our lives are not happened stance we did not just stumble into our blessing or lack of blessing. James Allen in his book "As a Man Thinketh" states "Every man is where he is by the *law of his being*, the *thoughts* which he has built into his character have brought him there, and in the arrangement of his life there is *no element of chance*, but all is *a result of a law* which cannot err. We have laws of thought that have been established in our subconscious that are implemented without us consciously thinking about them. James Allen challenges us to understand the laws of our thoughts. Our thoughts are laws! Rules that regulate the actions of our members (body, soul, and spirit). Meaning our thoughts have legal jurisdiction over our organs, health, and vitality; our character and who we are, and our spiritual beliefs, growth, development, and relationship with God. When we feel like we have violated our laws of thought, subconsciously, we impose penalties on ourselves. It is incumbent upon us to seek out and understand the laws of thoughts that we operate by because what we think in our heart/subconscious mind, we are!

CHAPTER 3

GETTING AN UNDERSTANDING

"Wisdom is the principal thing; Therefore, get wisdom. And in all your getting, get understanding."
— Proverbs 4:7 NKJV

"Wisdom is the application of knowledge!"
— Dr. Jerome Stokes

Being wise has is defined as having an understanding and good judgement. For most people, understanding and good judgement came by way of their experiences. With that, most young men have not been alive long enough to acquire a wealth of knowledge that comes by way of life experiences. So, the challenge is how as young men do we get wisdom and understanding that under normal circumstances can take a lifetime of experiences to acquire? Well, the first step is acknowledging we need wisdom and like King Solomon, ask of God. James 1:5 If any of you lacks wisdom, let him ask of God, who gives all liberally and without reproach, and it will be given to him. This is God's guarantee and promise to us. God says, ask and wisdom will be given without criticism. God is not giving us wisdom and calling us stupid in the process. He is helping us understand without making us pay for it through humiliation. The only requirement is that we ask in faith and do not waiver, just believe that God will hold to His promise to give us wisdom. Just as he did for King Solomon.

BECOMING A MAN, SON, KING & PREIST TODAY!

Hearing the story of the young King Solomon, becoming King at the age of 12 years old recognizing the need for God's wisdom before age 20, and as a young man asking God for wisdom to rule His people in 1 Kings 3. It is amazing to see how God honored his request and gave him wisdom to rule and to rule well, so much that the people marveled.

King Solomon understood that wisdom is principal! Wisdom is primary, first, foundational, foremost, and most important. So. instead of asking for money, women, or to be the best king ever, Solomon asked for wisdom to rule well! He knew he could not be successful at anything without understanding! **We can only rule what we understand! If we don't understand a thing, it will rule us!** At an appointed time, we will be overtaken by our ignorance.

After observing his father King David's relationship with God, Solomon realizes a few things.

1. God showed mercy to his father David, because David walked in truth and in righteousness and with an upright heart with God.
2. God gave David a son (Solomon) to sit on the throne.
3. Now as a young man with little understanding and many people to judge.

Solomon realized that he needed wisdom and a discerning heart to judge God's people. With that, he makes the request of God. The Lord responded to Solomon saying, "I have done according to your request. I have given you a wise and understanding heart."

This request is significant because as a King, Solomon does not have to answer anyone but God. Everyone listens to him and fears him. He can declare and decree laws, send men to war, and have everything placed at his feet. A King's wish is everyone's command. Yet, we find Solomon making a request for understanding. I imagine, Solomon looked back in retrospect at his father "King David's" ruling and relationship with God and realized to be good at this job, I must have wisdom because ignorance will not serve anyone well. Ignorant people cannot serve themselves, God, or God's people well.

Ignorance is not bliss!
— Willie G. Miller Jr.

As a young man task with judging God's people, Solomon needed understanding. I suggest that as young men in pursuit of mastering and ruling life, we need understanding. Having an understanding gives us the advantage and the ability to create greater opportunities for ourselves to be successful. I am not talking about a specific topic; I am speaking in general about any topic of interest as well as those that are basic to living life. For example, understanding yourself, home buying, budgeting, how to have good health, understanding the stock market or how to land a ship on the moon. You choose your area of interest, whatever it is, make sure you get an understanding of it.

Understanding this principle and applying it is important and vital to our lives. I am speaking of your natural and spiritual life. See, I realized, the Lord has fixed our lives to be bullet proof. I mean in a literal sense; we are bullet proof when we understand things pertaining to life and ourselves. When we give our lives over to the Lord and yield our vessels in service to the Kingdom, we are invincible. We become Supermen! There are two things that are our kryptonite. They **are not** sin and the devil but rather:

1. A lack of knowledge and
2. A lack of vision.

If we do not have knowledge and vision, we will sabotage our lives. The devil will not need to attack us; he can just stand back and watch us not succeed at life. People do not have to try to hold us back. Our lack of knowledge and vision will hold us back without them lifting a finger or having a thought against us. Knowledge is necessary!

**Without knowledge, destruction is inevitable.
Rejecting Knowledge = Rejecting God.**

Hosea 4:6 My people are destroyed for a lack of knowledge: because you have rejected knowledge, I will also reject you, that you shalt be no priest to me: seeing thou hast forgotten the law of thy God, I will also forget your children.

This is the voice of God speaking to His people; stating clear that His people are destroyed because of a lack of knowledge in general. Then the Lord switches the focus and makes it personal. When we reject knowledge, we are rejecting Him and then He will reject us. Not only us but our children. Wow! Seriously Lord? Yes! When we reject knowledge, we reject God!

Proverbs 1:7 The fear of the Lord is the beginning of knowledge, but fools despise wisdom and instruction. The foundation of knowledge is an understanding of the power and existence of God that leads us to a respectful fear of God. Which causes us to acknowledge Him and desire a relationship with Him that will cast down our fear. Our fear is exchanged for love (1 John 4:18). Such love has no fear because perfect love expels fear of punishment and shows that we have fully experienced his perfect love (New Living Translation).

As we evaluate our lives, we need to look at the areas where we lack knowledge because those areas become our kryptonite. We must also ensure that at the foundation of our knowledge must be an understanding of God and our need to be in relationship with Him. Otherwise, destruction awaits us on the other side of our ignorance.

No vision = Death!
Dreams Unwritten! = Dreams Unrealized!

Proverbs 29:18 Where there is no vision, the people perish: but he that keeps the law happy is he.

Having a vision for our life means we understand our purpose and mission in life. This means we have a picture in our minds of what our lives will look like in the future. A picture that we can put activities, actions, goals, and objectives in place for us to arrive at the image we have for our lives. Having a well thought out plan is essential. Otherwise, according to King Solomon, we will succumb to challenges in life because life's challenges can throw us off our course. So, if we have not charted our course, we will not remember how to find our way back on course when we are knocked off course. We might be blessed to achieve some successes; however, most unwritten dreams will not be realized and will die with us.

The vision we have for our lives must be written. Especially if we need help from others to achieve it. Habakkuk 2:2 And the Lord answered me, and said **write the vision, and make it plain** upon tables, that he may run who reads it. The runners need a picture of where they are running if they are going to help us achieve our vision. When we understand who we are and our purpose and mission in life, reading our written vision reminds us of it and helps to keep us on track to achieving our mission and purpose. A written vision gives life to what God has shown us about ourselves. Once you can see where you are heading, a well thought out plan is necessary. I am not talking about a one sentence statement. We must write clear plans with step-by-step instructions.

Cameron Herold in his book Vivid Vision said, "Imagine yourself inside of what you picture for your future. Touching it and experiencing it." Then he challenges us to explain what stands out about it and what we notice. Further, to describe what it looks like, how it feels, its features, lighting, the flow, energy and feel of it. Following this train of thought will require writing more than one sentence for our vision statement. When we do this, we will have what Cameron describes as a "Vivid Vision" that we and others can act on. Otherwise, life will deliver punches to our heads that can leave us bewildered, causing us to lose track of who we are and where we are going, all because we did not write it down.

If we want to be brilliant and extraordinary, we must get an understanding of who God is because that is the foundation of knowledge. Develop a love relationship with God that cast down fear of punishment. Understand who we are! Our purpose and the vision God have for our lives and write a clear explanation of what image we see for our future.

Knowledge and understanding are light!

Lacking knowledge is darkness! In one of his teachings on Kingdom, Dr. Myles Monroe stated: God is the first to rule by understanding (light)! The Devil is the first to rule by ignorance (darkness). When we enter things with an understanding, we are open to the rulership of God. We become less vulnerable to being overtaken by situations because we walk in the light of understanding which exposes hidden things. When we enter things that we are ignorant about, we are open to the rulership of the adversary, and we become as children inexperienced and vulnerable to being taken advantage of even to the point of losing our lives. We cannot afford to invite the Devil to our party because we lack knowledge. Instead, less get an understanding and invite the presence and light of God to the party of our lives.

We should always take a second to examine our lives to identify any areas where we are experiencing trouble and stagnation. If we look closer, we will find that the trouble areas are plaguing us because we lack an understanding of how to approach and deal with them.

Ephesians 4:27 teaches us to give no place to the Devil. Ignorance provides a place for the Devil to operate and bring darkness, disorder, and confusion into our lives. The light of understanding invites God into our situation and closes the door to demonic influence.

Getting an understanding is key. We can only master and control what we can comprehend. If we aspire to know God, we need to get an understanding about Him. If we want to have a vision for our life, we must get an understanding about who we are. If we want to invest our money, we must get an understanding about investing. If we want a better relationship. We must get an understanding. If we want to have our own businesses, get an understanding.

King Solomon said, when we exalt understanding, understanding will promote us. If we embrace understanding, understanding will bring us honor. Understanding will bring an ornament of grace and a crown of glory to our heads (Proverbs 4:8-9).

CHAPTER 4

HOW TO SPEAK

Thou shalt also decree a thing, and it shall be
> established unto thee: and the light shall shine
> upon thy ways.
>
> — Job 22:28

A man's belly shall be satisfied with the fruit of his mouth; and with the increase of his lips shall he be filled. Death and life are in the power of the tongue: and they that love it shall eat the fruit thereof. These are the words of King David out of Proverbs 18:20-21. In the article "Holy Spirit", Caitlyn Lutz defines the belly as the heart of a man. Representing the seat of our emotions and our deepest inner parts. Meaning that the words that proceed out of our mouths are fruit or nourishment to our hearts, our emotions, and our deepest inner parts.

If we release positive words, our heart receives fresh fruit that produces life. If we release negative words, our heart receives rotten fruit which produces death. Our self-talk is just as important as the words we speak to others. In our relationship with ourselves and others, we need to watch what we say because with our mouths we can produce life and/or death.

We must make a conscience effort to guard what comes out of our mouths. As a young man, I would not let people say just anything to me any kind of way. I wanted them to show respect in the way they spoke to me. As an adult, I hold myself accountable to the same standard. I will not allow myself to speak words to me that will not produce life. If I have a moment of bad self-talk, I ask myself to whom are you talking? I check and correct myself by reminding myself that I must respect and manage myself properly with honor. I do not talk to myself when I am not in proper headspace emotionally. I sit quietly and think then I release the proper fruit from my lips that will produce life. I refuse to have a premature death of my ideas, God's promises or of my natural life because of loose lips that release loose declarations. The scripture says that we shalt also decree a thing, and it shall be established to us. The term "loose lips sink ships" is applicable here.

As men, we must operate with ourselves based in understanding. Prudent interaction with ourselves and others is critical to our success. The cost for dealing with ourselves and others foolishly is great. Proverbs 18:6-7 say a fool's mouth is his destruction and his lips are a snare of his soul. A fool's lips create a trap for his soul. His emotions and intellect become captive to the foolishness that proceeds from his mouth. This speaks to the internal damage caused by foolish conversation. There are natural and physical implications to foolish talk. Foolish conversation causes heated disagreements that lead to a person fighting and hitting you. With our spoken words, we can change the trajectory of our lives quickly for the positive or negative.

Our words are us!

In the beginning was the Word, and the Word was with God, and the Word was God (John 1:1). Looking at this verse of scripture helps us understand that our words are us. Men cannot be separated from the words that proceed from their mouths. Our words are with us, and they are us. Our words are spiritually alive.

Our words go before us to create!

When released into the atmosphere, our spoken words can create things that do not yet appear. We are made in the likeness and image of God. Just as God spoke all of creation into existence, we can speak things into existence. When coupled with faith, our words can move mountains. Matthew 17:20-21 speaks of this and goes a little further. Jesus says when we exercise our faith by speaking to mountains, they will move from one place to another, he completes his statement by adding that nothing will be impossible for us. When we see the results of our words coupled with our faith, we will start believing God for anything. We will begin to speak to everything around us and nothing will be impossible. Faith begets Faith!

Jay-Z embodied this position in his interview with Dean Baquet of the New York Times. When asked if he had an opportunity to talk to those, he sold drugs to and caused pain as a young man, before Jay-Z could respond, Dean Baquet said, what would you say to them or is that impossible? Jay-Z's first response was, "no, and nothing is impossible, right!" The interview continued, however, I sat for a minute and thought about Jay-Z's unflinching, calm confidence on display as he responded, "RIGHT!" expecting the interviewer to validate his spoken position that nothing is impossible.

His spoken words create an atmosphere where he can accomplish anything he sets out to accomplish. You have the same ability.

Our words can become flesh and dwell among us!

The Word was made flesh, and dwelt among us, (and we beheld his glory, the glory as of the only begotten of the Father,) full of grace and truth. John 1:14 is speaking of God's word becoming flesh and living in body among us in the form of Jesus Christ. I know, you are thinking God's words are not our words. Let me remind you, we are made in the likeness and image of God. Meaning we have like or similar qualities. For example, when parents speak negatively to their children. Telling them that they will never be anything. The children take those negative comments and live their lives never becoming anything great. While on the other hand, a parent can tell a child that one day they will be the president of the United States. That child will live their lives on purpose with intention and before you know, they are elected to be president. Your words are spirit, and they can be deposited into others around you. Watch what you say because once your words are released, they can shape the lives of those around you.

CHAPTER 5

BECOMING A SON

But as many as received him, to them gave he power to become the sons of God, even to them that believe on his name: Which were born, not of blood, nor of the will of the flesh, nor of the will of man, but of God.
— John 1: 12-13

One of the joyful and rewarding benefits of the fathering dimension is that it produces the Spirit of sonship unto full maturity and spiritual inheritance of ministry in Love, Leadership, and Legacy through divinely appointed Lineage.
— Apostle Tim Early

Sonship is a gift from God that is received through our faith in Jesus Christ. It is reserved for those who are born of God and led of God.

There was a Pharisee by the name of Nicodemus who came to Jesus at night. He told Jesus you must come from God because no one could perform the miracles you performed accept God was with him. Jesus responded to Nicodemus, you must be born again, or you cannot enter heaven. Nicodemus stated, I cannot enter my mother womb to be born again! Jesus responds, not of flesh and blood, rather of water and the spirit (John 3:1-21). Nicodemus, your spirit man must be quickened by the spirit of God.

God is Spirit. If we want to relate to Him, we must do it with our spirit man. Jeus told Nicodemus, flesh gives birth to flesh but the Spirit "God" gives birth to the spirit. Because God *is* Spirit, and those who worship Him must worship in spirit and truth." John 4:24

When we receive God, and believe on the name of Jesus Christ, we are born again. At that moment, God gives us the *power to become* the Sons of God. Meaning, we are not sons yet. Rather, we have the *right and authority* to change our behavior and act in a certain way. God gives us power to change our behavior and choose to be *led by the Spirit*. For those who are led by the Spirit of God, they are the sons of God. Romans 8:14

Sonship is powerful. We call God Father because we have received the Spirit of adoption. The Spirit of God bears witness to our spirit that we are the children of God. The Spirit of God testifies to our spirit that we are sons of God. God shows to us that sonship is true, and it really exist it our relationship with Him. It is very important we learn to be led by the Spirit of God. If we are not those who are led of God, we cannot be Sons. The Spirit of God guides us into all truth (John 16:13).

Sonship is demonstrated throughout the bible. Whenever God is going to use a person in the earth, he makes sure a father relationship is established to prepare the man or woman of God. For example: Moses had Pharoah. David had King Saul. Elisha had Elijah. The disciples had Jesus. Timothy had Paul.

The model of sonship has been demonstrated throughout the bible. Even when least expected, God takes one of His men of the hour and place them in a position with adversarial forces to be groom for the work of God. We saw it in the life of Joseph when he was in Potiphar's house. Potiphar gave Joseph responsibilities that prepared him to be second in command in Egypt during a time of famine. God used Joseph to save the house of Jacob a.k.a. Israel. Look closely, you will see the pattern of Love, Leadership, and Legacy through divinely appointed Lineage.

The same truth holds in the life of Moses. While all the boy babies were being killed in Egypt, God saved Moses and shortly after, used him to deliver His people. Moses was taken from the water by the Pharoah's daughter. He was taken (adopted) into the household of the King. He was groomed and taught aspects of leadership. Later he killed a man and was led into exile to the house of Jethro where he learned how to be a shepherd. Again, a father figure taught Moses how to care for the lost sheep of Israel. Moses was adopted as a child and again as a man. He was taught how to lead and care for God's people. Eventually, leading them out of the hands of Egyptian hardship into a land flowing with milk and honey.

One of the greatest examples of Love, Leadership, and Legacy through divinely appointed Lineage is the story of King David, the son of Jesse of the tribe of Judah.

The story begins with Saul of the tribe of Benjamin as King of Isreal. King Saul decided to go against the commandments of God. As a result, God used the prophet Samuel to pronounce His judgment upon King Saul. Samuel told King Saul, since you have done foolishly, his reign as King will not continue. Samuel further explained that God was seeking a man after His heart and has commanded that man to be captain over His people (1 Samuel 13:13-14).

Love in Sonship

God was attracted to David because David loved Him. David had a selfless connection with God that transcend circumstances and was rooted in unwavering commitment to serving God. David was a shepherd boy who tended to his father's sheep and a musician who loved writing, singing and playing songs to the glory of God. So, when we speak of love, it's not just God's love toward us as sons but also our love towards Him as a Father that positions us to be blessed and used by Him.

God's love for us is demonstrated for us in that while we were still sinners, Christ died for us (Romans 5:8). Also, the bible declares says, that God so loved the world that he gave his only begotten Son, that whoever believes in him should not perish but have eternal life" (John 3:16). Yes, it seems like King David was born and lived before Jesus Christ was crucified for us. You must understand, Jesus was crucified before the foundation of the world (Revelation 13:7-9). God's love for us was expressed in His preparedness to respond to Adams's mistake in the garden of Eden, eating fruit from the forbidden tree before Adam was formed from the dust of the earth. God's love for us was already predetermined. He already decided for Jesus to die for our sins so that we could have a relationship with Him and become sons. Love is reciprocal! We express our love towards God by chasing after Him with our heart and He expresses His love towards us by coming and residing in us in the form of the Holy Spirit. Right after Samuel anointed David to be King, the Spirit of the Lord came upon him from that day forward (1Samuel 16:13). The English Standard Version (ESV) states, the spirit of the Lord rushed upon David from that day forward. God stands ready to partner with us in a love relationship as our Father to accomplish His will in the earth.

Leadership in Sonship

David was anointed king when he was 15-16 years old. Shortly after, he was called upon to minister to King Saul because the Spirit of the Lord departed from Saul and a harmful spirit from the Lord tormented him. David was skillful upon instruments and would play for King Saul when the tormenting spirit from God would be upon him. When David played the tormenting spirit from God would leave and King Saul would be well and refreshed. Immediately, David was given access to the King by God's divine providence.

Later, when King Saul was faced with Goliath, David shows up with food for his brothers. When David heard that Goliath was defying God, he questioned those around about want would happen for the person who killed Goliath, they responded, the king will enrich the man who kills him with great riches and will give him his daughter and make his father's house free in Israel. David's brothers approached him bringing accusations and sarcastic comments. David ignored the distractions of his brothers and moved with purpose.

1. David understood *the battle was God's*.
2. *He knew what was in it for him* - the reward for being used by God to kill Goliath.
3. *He was not distracted* - by family members who could not see his potential and were jealous because he was anointed to be king.

King Saul heard what David said, he called for him. King Saul cautioned David that he did not have the experience of Goliath. Goliath was trained to fight and war from a young age. David leaned on his own experience with God. He testified to the King that when the lion and bear came for his sheep, he struck them down, and just like he struck them down, he will strike Goliath down because he has defied the armies of the living God.

Saul gave David his armor. David said I have not tested this armor. I have tested my sling and rocks. I will go with what God has made me successful with in the past.

4. David had *no fear because he had his testimony*.
5. David *went in the strength of how God uses him*.

David meets Goliath on the battlefield. David stated, you come to me with sword, spear and a javelin but I come to you in the name of the Lord, the God of the armies of Isreal, whom you have defiled. David declares this day I will strike you down and cut off your head and I will give the dead bodies of the host of the philistines this day to the birds of the air and the wild beast of the earth, that all the earth will know that there is a God in Isreal. 1 Samuel 17:41-53.

David defeats Goliath.

At a young age, God led and inspired David while tending his father's sheep. Later, we see this Youngman through his faith and belief in God inspire and influence others toward a shared vision of defeating Goliath and the Philistine armies. God showed David in the wilderness that the attacks against the sheep were attacks against His God. David showed the armies of Israel that it was God's fight and that if anyone comes against God no matter how big they are, they will fall. By giving David, the skill to kill the lion and the bear, God empowered David to stand up to and kill Goliath. By killing Goliath, David created an environment where others could feel empowered to contribute and thrive. Immediately following Goliath's death, the armies of Isreal were inspired and empowered to pursue and kill all the Philistines.

Legacy through Sonship

After being anointed king and the spirit of the Lord coming upon David, he began his journey to establishing his legacy through sonship. King David will forever be known as the man after God's own heart. A man who frequently sought divine guidance from God. A man of war who relied on God for his tactical skills to ensure his success. A King who lived to see God's promises realized. He was God's instrument in securing Israel's borders, establishing peace and paving the way for Solomon's reign.

King David's life was full of complications, family challenges, and on different occasions, he let God down. However, he left a legacy that impacts us today. His values and contributions are felt by many today as they look to the Psalms for inspiration, revelation and prophet releases that have been fulfilled at the coming of Jesus Christ. He left an indelible mark on the world that continues to touch generations and influence our worship experience and relationship with God.

David was a warrior-king, and his military campaigns and wins are a testament to his reliance on God and his ability to execute on what God gives him to do. The bible does not give an account of all his battles. However, here is a record of his victories:

1. Defeating Goliath – one-on-one fight marking the beginning of David's rise to King (1 Samuel 17).
2. Multiple battles against the Philistines
    a. Victories under King Saul as a commander (1 Samuel 18:5-30).
    b. After becoming King (2 Samuel 5:17-25).
3. The Battle for Jerusalem (2 Samuel 5:6-10). He captured the Jebusites stronghold.

4. Various Wars Against Neighboring Nations. David expanded Israels territory and influence:
   - Moabites: He defeated Moab and made them vassals (2 Samuel 8:2).
   - Ammonites: David waged a successful war against Ammon after they insulted his envoys (2 Samuel 10).
   - Arameans (Syrians): He subdued the Aramean kingdoms (2 Samuel 8:3-8).
   - Edomites: David conquered Edom and established control over them (2 Samuel 8:13-14).
5. Civil Conflicts
   - Against Saul's Forces: While fleeing from Saul, David had minor skirmishes but refrained from directly harming Saul.
   - Absalom's Rebellion: David fought to reclaim his throne after his son Absalom led a revolt (2 Samuel 18).
   - Sheba's Revolt: David quelled a rebellion led by Sheba, son of Bichri (2 Samuel 20).

Sonship through Divinely Appointed Lineage

David's victory over Goliath landed him a place to live with King Saul in the palace. Additionally, David and King Saul's son Johnathan made a covenant because he loved him as he loved himself. Shortly following, Johnathan stripped himself of the robe that was upon him and gave it to David, and his garments, even his sword, and his bow, and to his girdle. (1 Samuel 18:1-4).

Historically, the thrones of Kings were reserved for their sons. It seems likely, that if King Saul was the reigning king of Isreal that scepter would pass to one of his sons. In this case, Johnathan. Even more interesting, King Saul was from the tribe of Benjamin. So, if not Johnathan, someone from the tribe of Benjamin would more likely be heir to the throne of King Saul. Under normal circumstances, all these questions would come to mind. However, in this case, God had predetermined that the scepter would not depart from Judah.

Fourteen generations before David was born, his forefather Jacob established this prophetic blessing over Judah and his seed (Genesis 49:10). David is from the lineage and ancestral chain of Judah thereby a beneficiary of divinely appointed lineage. David becoming King was established fourteen generations before David was born. The Father and Son relationship that God had with Jacob continues to benefit Jacob's lineage. Jacob demonstrated this relationship with his sons as he speaks a blessing over them that God honors because of Jacob's relationship with Him. This is powerful because later in David's life, God established the Davidic Covenant – a promised made to David in the Bible that a descendant of David would rule the people of God forever (2 Samuel 7:8-16) and mentioned in Psalms 89:3-4 and 132:11-12. David grew to know God as his father. In fact, in Psalms 2:7, David proclaimed what God decreed: God said to me, "You are my son; and today have become your father."

Now, fourteen generations later, David of the tribe of Judah is standing in the house of King Saul of the tribe of Benjamin. Anointed to be the next King over

Isreal with no natural ties to the throne. He would need to be adopted by King Saul to be his son to have access to the throne. That was not likely to happen because King Saul grew to hate David and was bitter because he knew David was God's choice to take the throne. In fact, King Saul pursued David for a long time trying to take his life.

God always has way of accomplishing what His will is. King Saul's son Johnathan loved David and made a covenant with David. Also, Johnathan gave David all his royal clothing. The robe, tunic, and weapons that Jonathan gave David are symbols of his position as the son of the king and heir to the throne. By giving these items to David, Jonathan is not just acknowledging their covenant to one another in friendship but also acknowledging that David is the one chosen by God to lead Israel.

Jonathan's robe identified Jonathan as a prince. Wherever he went wearing that robe, everyone knew he was royalty with all the privileges and authority that came with the distinction. By giving David his robe, Jonathan bestowed on him prince-hood, brotherhood, and sonship. He no longer considered him a mere shepherd, but royalty, a prince and son of a King! Johnathan also gave him the shirt off his back. Meaning he did not mind if David was mistaken for being him. Johnathan gave up his identity as prince and placed it onto David (Powers, 2013). Jonathan's gift was not just a material exchange; it was a profound spiritual act of submission, love, and recognition of God's anointing on David and provided David a natural right to the throne of King Saul. What God established in the spiritual realm has entered the natural realm. David was a beneficiary of adoption into the family of King Saul through his son Johnathan.

After being anointed king, it took approximately thirteen years for David to ascend to the throne and become king of Israel. David spent a significant amount of time on the run as a fugitive, fleeing from Saul. However, God's promise was realized as we transition into the new testament, Matthew 1, we read the genealogy (lineage) of Jesus the Messiah, looking at Matthew 1:6. We see King David included in the lineage of Jesus Christ - and Jesse the father of *King David*. David was the father of Solomon, whose mother had been Uriah's wife. Jesus Christ is King of kings and Lord of lords, and his Kingdom is an everlasting Kingdom.

Luke 1:31-33

> And, behold, thou shalt conceive in thy womb, and bring forth a son, and shalt call his name Jesus.
>
> He shall be great, and shall be called the Son of the Highest: and the Lord God shall give unto him the throne of his father David:
>
> And he shall reign over the house of Jacob forever; and of his kingdom there shall be no end.

The Lord desires that we practice the same model of Sonship in our interaction with our children. It does not end there, He is looking for us to make and father sons in the Kingdom. Leaders in the body of Christ cannot be self-centered and short minded. We must become fathers, embrace the Spirit of Sonship, and create a spiritual inheritance in our ministries that is anchored in love, leadership, and legacy through divinely appointed lineage.

CHAPTER 6

BECOMING A KING

After this manner therefore pray ye: Our Father which art in heaven, Hallowed be thy name. Thy kingdom come, Thy will be done on earth, as it is in heaven. Give us this day our daily bread. And forgive us our debts, as we forgive our debtors. And lead us not into temptation but deliver us from evil: For thine is the kingdom, and the power, and the glory, forever. Amen.

— Matthew 6:9-13

You yourselves have seen what I did to Egypt, and how I carried you on eagles' wings and brought you to myself. Now if you obey me fully and keep my covenant, then out of all nations you will be my treasured possession. Although the whole earth is mine, you will be for me a kingdom of priests and a holy nation. These are the words you are to speak to the Israelites.

— Exodus 19:4-6 NIV

Understanding the position that Jesus Christ's sacrifice has purchased for us, provides the foundational principles which our lives are established as Men of God. Jesus is a King and Priest after the order of Melchizedek and we are His sons so, we are King Priests after the order of Melchizedek. Over the next two chapters, we are going to explore what it means to be a King Priest.

God has given MAN a Kingdom called EARTH!

We opened this chapter with the Lord's prayer because it shines light on what believers should be praying for and what we should be focusing on. In fact, if you read a few verses ahead, Jesus is admonishing his disciples to not pray in vain repetitions with much speaking. Rather, pray as He instructs them:

1. Jesus establishes where God our Father is – in heaven.
2. That God's name is holy, consecrated and should be respected.
3. Then Jesus prays for the Kingdom of God to come to the earth!
4. That God's will be done in the earth as it is in heaven.

Jesus makes it clear that God is in heaven because He wants us to understand that jurisdictional authority over the earth has been given to man. Yes, the earth is the Lord's and the fullness thereof; the world, and those who dwell therein (Psalms 24:1). However, man is in charge and responsible for directing and coordinating operations in the earth. We dominate the systems of the world; however, we do not dominate one another.

God said, Let us make man in our image, after our likeness: and ***let them have dominion*** over the fish of the sea, and over the fowl of the air, and over the cattle, and over all the earth, and over every creeping thing that creeps upon the earth (Genesis 1:26). Jesus establishes that God is not residing here in the earth because He left man in charge to rule and have dominion.

Next, Jesus informs us God is holy and that His name should be respected. God expects us to have an approach to Him that suggests we have respect and reverence for who He is. The Apostle Peter reminds us, that God who called us is holy, so we should be holy in all manner of conversation because it is written, be ye holy; for I am holy (1Peter 1:15-17).

Next, Jesus gives us a glimpse into the invisible realms and the mind of God when he instructs us to pray that the Kingdom and will of God be done in the earth as it is in heaven. If a Kingdom is in heaven, there must be a King! There cannot be a Kingdom without a King. So, God is a King! A King with a Kingdom in heaven that he wants to expand into the earth!

God has a Kingdom that He wants to expand into the earth.

When Jesus prays for the Kingdom of God to come to the earth and that God's will is done in the earth as it is in heaven, He brings awareness to mankind that God has a Kingdom in heaven, and He desires that His Kingdom comes to the earth. In Jesus prayer, He opens our eyes to God's original intent to expand His Kingdom into the earth. God is a King and Kings expand and take territory. Then, they establish government by placing a representative in the territory to establish and ensure that the culture and government of the new territory duplicates the culture of their

Kingdom. In this case, the culture and government of the earth should duplicate heavens.

The Bible is about a King and a Kingdom!

— Dr. Myles Monroe

God created the heavens and the earth. Then He made man in His likeness and image and gave us dominion over the earth to rule and govern. God intended on having a relationship with mankind to establish His Kingdom in the earth. However, Adam's inability to be holy as God is holy; caused him to yield to Satan's influence. In disobedience to God, Adam partook of the fruit of the tree of knowledge of good and evil. Thereby, forfeiting His birthright as a King and losing what he inherited as an heir of God. His position as a son of God and his Kingship. He lost access to the territory that God established for Him to rule over and establish right order. Ultimately, Adam lost his authority to establish the Kingdom of heaven on the earth.

Jesus came to put us back on track with God's original intent to expand His Kingdom into the earth. He came to restore us back into our rightful position with God so that we can know the heart of God and bring the Kingdom of Heaven to the earth! Jesus is so intentional about this that His first message was "Repent for the Kingdom of Heaven is at hand" (Mathew 3:2). Metanoia is Greek for repent. Meaning to change your mind set from anything else that you have heard and open your mind to the Kingdom of Heaven. Jesus is saying, I am coming with new wine, and it cannot be poured into old wineskins (Mathew 9:17).

You cannot pour the new wine concept of the Kingdom of Heaven into old religious wineskins of the religious sects of that day or of this day. It is not about denominations; it is about a King and a Kingdom! Dr. Miles Monroe said, "Jesus did not come to establish a religion, He came to introduce a Kingdom. He did not come to repair a religion; He came to restore Kings."

God had to come in the body of Jesus Christ to redeem us back to Himself and restore our birthright. To redeem suggests that we belonged to Him and He wanted to regain possession of us in exchange for His life as payment for Adam's sin that he brought on us all.

Remember, God gave mankind dominion in the earth. He gave us jurisdictional authority. So, the only way you can have jurisdictional authority on the earth is you need to have an earthen vessel. To operate on the earth, you must have a body. God enrolled Himself in a body of flesh to restore us back into fellowship with Him. If we receive him, he gives us power to become the sons of God (John 1:12). As a son of God, we are sons of a King. By birthright, we are kings and lords! There by making God "King of kings and Lord of lords" (Revelation 14:14).

You are KING! A King with a "Kingdom of Heaven" mandate to bring the Kingdom of Heaven into the earth. We are not kings who seek to build our thrones and take territory for our own selfish agendas. No! Rather, we seek first the Kingdom of God and his righteousness and know that all other things will be added to us (Matthew 6:33). Our purpose is to expand the Kingdom of Heaven onto the earth!

God's Kings Receive Power.

God promises that you will receive power, after the Holy Spirit comes upon you (Acts 1:8). When you decide to change your mindset (repent) and received God and the Kingdom of Heaven, you will receive power! Kings need power to establish their Kingdom. Surely, you will need God's power to establish His Kingdom on the earth.

Do not worry, the Holy Spirit is our helper, advisor, mediator, legal defender, and advocate. He will provide what is needed to complete the work of God. He does not just come along side us; He comes to reside inside of us. Apostle Paul asks the church at Corinth, did you not know that you are the temple or building of God, and that the Spirit of God dwells in you (1Corinthians 3:16)?

One of the greatest smuggling acts that occurred during the history of mankind was God in us alive in the form of His Holy Spirit. I believe Satan would have left Jesus alone if he knew that after Jesus laid down his life, He would return and live in us in the form of His holy spirit. Well, it is too late now, it is finished! Now we have a comforter which is the Holy Spirit that was sent from our Father in Jesus name, who teaches us all things and brings all things to our remembrance that we have heard Jesus say out of the Bible (John 14:26).

The Holy Spirit gives us heaven's perspective. God speaks to us through His Holy Spirit and provides us glimpses into what He thinks and what He would do in the situations and scenarios that we face as His Kings. We must be confident that God is with us because we are tasked with the clever work of establishing the Kingdom of Heaven in the earth so that God's will can be done. This is not an easy undertaking. It can seem overwhelming because we are in the process of learning about God and establishing a relationship with Him while at the same time, implementing on tasks that express His will, His culture, and power in the earth.

This process can seem daunting because there are so many things we do not know. We do not know what we do not know. – David T. Stokes. The bible declares that we know in part and prophesy in part (1 Corinthians 13:9). I encourage you today that God has thought about our lack of knowledge and has provided us with a comforter in the form of the Holy Spirit that leads and guides us into all truth by speaking to us things that He hears from God (John 16:14).

Kingship!

Jesus was born a King. We are born into Kingship. We become Kings by our birthright. This is not a fleshly birthright. It is a spiritual birthright. A Pharisee named Nicodemus came to talk to Jesus at night. Nicodemus said, Jesus, we know you are a teacher from God because you do all these miracles, and no one would be able to do these miracles without God. Jesus cut to the chase, responding to Nicodemus saying truly I say to you, you must be born again. Born of the spirit. Otherwise, you cannot see the Kingdom of God. Nicodemus, your spiritual man must be born again. Made alive to the things of God. (John 3:1-21)

When our spirit man is quickened and made alive by the holy spirit, we become new creatures in Christ. We become spiritual sons of God. Making us Kings! Making God, King of kings (Matthew 24:32). Now, we must do what Kings do!

Kings own territory and property.

The story of David and Goliath was about a Philistine King wanting to take territory from God's people through war. They were at a stale mate because King Saul did not have any men in his Kingdom to fight against Goliath. If the wrong man went out to fight Goliath and lost, King Saul would lose his kingdom. The territory and everything in it including natural and human resources. David standing up against Goliath and killing him was major because if he lost, God's people would succumb to the Philistines and be at the mercy of the Philistine King (1 Samuel 17).

God gives kings territory to possess and to own. As kings, we must maintain possession of the territory, or we cannot exercise the mandate of God in that territory. If we lose the territory, we lose authorization from God to act on His behalf in that territory. We lose the right to exercise an order or commission granted by God to us for the establishment of a heavenly government over that territory.

If we are not owners of the land, we are strangers, and the land does not receive us. It does not matter how long we are in the territory, if we don't own it, the territory sees us as strangers. That is why home and land ownership is important. If we rent space, the owner has the right to move us out and occupy the space when they are ready to do whatever they want to do.

This principle applies to spiritual realms more than the natural. When my former church purchased new space to build a larger sanctuary, my pastor shared a story of the time he had to face the principality over the new property/territory. God opened his eyes so he could see the adversarial forces that were fighting to hold on to that territory. Even though the building was financially purchased, and the building project was underway, that prince had to be uprooted in the realm of the spirit before we could occupy the space. Once the stronghold over the territory was removed, we occupied the space and began to have services, and many lives were saved in that territory.

Kings Know Their Territory.

To rule well, Kings must understand the boundaries of their territory. In the movie Lion King, Mufasa takes his son Simba up on a high mount to show Him his territory. "He tells Simba, "Everything the light touches is our Kingdom." Further, Mufasa tells Simba not to go to the Elephant Graveyard, it is forbidden territory beyond the borders of the Pride lands." Kings are not called to rule another's territory. However, you have complete authority and rule over what is yours. There is territory that God has given each of us. It is incumbent upon us to know where it is and possess it!

Kings Take Territory.

When we examine the Old Testament, quickly we are made aware that God is about Kingdom of Heaven expansion in the earth. King David's conquest created the largest borders Isreal ever had. At that time, up to 60,000 square miles. During his reign, King David was a territory-taking warrior king. The Bible does not give an exact count of the number of times David took territory, but it does document at least seven times David took or reclaimed territories.

Transitioning into the New Testament, as King, Jesus took a different approach. Remember, in Jesus first message, He told the people to repent for the Kingdom of Heaven is at hand. Later when the disciples asked how they should pray Jesus responded, Our Father who art in heaven, hollowed be thy name, thy KINGDOM come, thy WILL be done in the earth as in HEAVEN. Jesus told the disciples in John 14:26 But the Comforter, which is the Holy Ghost, whom the Father will send in my name, he shall teach you all things, and bring all things to your remembrance, whatsoever I have said unto you.

Jesus is saying, instead of you physically going to take territory, after I lay down my life, the father is going to put Himself inside of you and He is going to teach you and remind you of the things I said to you. God has put His holy spirit inside of every believer across the world. So, everywhere a believer is, God is in that believer giving them Kingdom of Heaven perspective to release in the territory that they occupy.

What we are witnessing is God making good on promises that He made to our forefathers. He promised Abraham He will multiply his seed as the stars of the heaven and as the sand, which is upon the seashore, and in thy seed shall all nations be blessed (Genesis 22:17). People from all around the world who are saved are considered the seed of Abraham. Also, God kept a prophetic promise that He made to Moses with Joshua. Telling Joshua that every place that the sole of your foot walks upon, that have I given unto you, as I said unto Moses (Joshua 1:3-6). That means as the spiritual ancestors of Abraham and Moses, the same prophecy applies to us today. So, that means that Christians all over the world wherever they walk, God has given them that place/territory.

As Kings, based solely on the prophetic word of God, we take territory to establish the Kingdom of Heaven, simply by allowing our feet to touch the territory. On your job, that is spiritually your territory. In your apartment complex, that is your territory. In your home and neighborhood, that is your territory. Wherever your feet walk is your territory. It may be hard to wrap your thinking around that God is King and as his sons we become kings, and that the nature of Kings is to take and possess territory! Well, let it settle in, we are Kings on assignment in the earth to expand the Kingdom of Heaven.

When we take territory, we establish Kingdom culture by speaking the word of God and carrying the spirit of God into the territory walking with boldness. We bring peace and love into the territory and enforce it against all adversarial forces. That means like Gideon, we might need to tear down the old altars that have been established to foreign gods and build new ones to the glory of the one true and living God. Like Nehemiah, we might need to rebuild walls of reclaimed territory. Like David, we might need to worship God and war at the same time. Whatever it takes because we understand, we were born to take territory with power and authority. Wherever we go, we take Kingdom with us. We don't shrink! We don't settle! We don't surrender! We step in with authority standing in victory and take it! In Jesus name!

Kings Have Glory.

A King's glory is expressed in their nature which is our life, personality, and character. This is demonstrated in the way Kings think, feel, and behave. God has planted gifts and talents in each person. These gifts and talents are God's glory in us concealed. When we use these gifts and talents to achieve great works and significant achievements, our glory is recognized by others, celebrated and sometimes rewarded.

When we accept Christ into our lives, we take on the mind of Christ (Philippians 2:5-6). Our acceptance of Christ becomes an expression of our new mindset which is demonstrated in the way we establish Kingdoms. The nature of God is expressed through our lives, personality and character. Our kingdom looks like God's Kingdom. When people interact with us, they experience the Kingdom of Heaven on the earth. The atmosphere of our homes and territory become the express nature of God.

A Kings Power is Unlimited

When we operate in the power of the holy spirit as kings, our power is unlimited. We receive power when the holy Spirit comes upon us. Power to become witnesses and boldness to act on what we believe. Power to house and release the power of the Holy Spirit to heal, deliver and set captives free.

As Apostle Peter approach the gate called beautiful, a lame man request silver or gold. Peter responded, "I do not have silver or gold (Acts 3:2-8). However, I have the power of the Holy Spirit to give. With that, Peter told the lame man to take up his bed and walk." As Kings, we operate with that same power. The infinite power of the Holy Spirit that can be released to bring healing and deliverance and to establish the kingdom and will of God in the earth.

Kings Establish Right Order.

The word of a king is the law in his kingdom territory. What you say matters. You cannot separate a man from their word. Your word is your bond. John 1:1-5 states; in the beginning was the Word, and the Word was with God, and the Word was God. Your word is you! Making you and your words powerful.

It is critical that you understand that you are establishing God's Kingdom in the earth in territory that He has given you as part of your kingdom. He is the King of kings. As such, in our territory, we are agents of the Kingdom of Heaven. We observe God's covenant and laws. We are divinely chosen of God to rule on His behalf in the earth. God's word in us is the law in the territory that He has blessed us with.

A Kings Territory Testifies to God.

Territory testifies to God what happens on it. Cain killed his brother Abel. The Lord said to Cain, where is Abel, your brother? Cain responded, "I do not know. Am I my brother's keeper?" The Lord responds to Cain, asking what have you done? The voice of thy brother's blood cries to me from the ground (Genesis 4:9-10). The earth offers testimony to God about what happens on it.

When taking territory, we must establish a higher covenant with God above anything that has happened before on the ground. When we purchased our new home, we buried bibles under the corners of the house, at every doorway of the house and at the entry point under the driveway. We established a higher covenant with God that superseded any that may have been established before we arrived. We prayed over the land and the house and declared and decreed that it is "A Place Called Blessed!" We established this land and home a place that will bear witness to how awesome, great, and mighty our God is. That is how we established - RIGHT ORDER!

The proclamations and decrees of a king are irrefutable and unmovable.

As kings, God has given us the power to decree a thing. Job 22:28 states; thou shalt decree a thing, and it shall be established unto you: and the light shall shine upon thy ways. As kings, what we say matters. We must watch what we say. No loose lip declarations. Our words are always looking for a place to be planted so they can live. God's words became flesh and dwelled among us in the world in the body of Jesus Christ. As with God's words, our words are looking for someone to reside in so they can become flesh and dwell among mankind.

When we speak, our words are established and come to pass. We have the ability with our spoken word to bring life or death. Proverbs 18:20-22 tells us a man's belly shall be satisfied with the fruit of his mouth; and with the harvest of his lips shall he be filled because death and life are in the power of the tongue, and they that love it shall eat the fruit thereof. We cannot call our wives and children crazy names and expect them to be anything other than what we have declared over them. We cannot tell them negative things that will cause them to live their lives based on the curses we released over them. They will become products of our poor kingship and territory. Our territory must be like God's. A kingdom of heaven territory filled with the love of God as described in 1 Corinthians 13.

The Reputation of a Kings is determined by the state of their Kingdom.

When the righteous are in authority, the people rejoice: but when the wicked have rule, the people mourn (Proverbs 29:2). As kings, we must understand that we rule by divine authority and that Jesus is central in practice and His presence is not optional. Jesus's presence is the priority. His voice in us sets the order and the direction and vision of our kingdom.

A healthy kingdom is not just rich in human and natural resources. It is rich in righteousness that refers to God's inherent justice, holiness, and moral perfection. It is established in order based on the biblical directive, found in Corinthians 14:40 "let all things be done decently and in order". It is established in love because love never fails (1 Corinthians 13). If we want to have an everlasting and unfailing Kingdom, love must be the foundation upon which we are building. Our Kingdom must be built on freedom that is expressed in the nature and heart of God. God has declared that whom the son sets free is free indeed. We do not rule in our territory over one another. We dominate over adversarial forces not one another.

Jesus is honored and He is at the center of all that we say and do. He is seated on the throne of our hearts and minds. He is not just our savior, He is our Lord and King therefore, decisions are not made by popular vote but by divine direction that proceeds from the throne room of our hearts where Jesus is seated. As a healthy kingdom, the throne of our heart is never empty.

In our kingdom, there is a culture of love and honor, not hierarchy. We provide a safe place for the people of God to grow, be free to serve, and to respond to the call of greatness. Joy is not optional; it is our strength. Peace is not circumstantial; it is a principle. Jesus said, "Peace I leave with you, my peace I give unto you: not as the world giveth, give I unto you.

Let not your heart be troubled, neither let it be afraid." (John 14:27)

In our kingdom, there is no competition; everyone cooperates, and identities are affirmed. We see who God has called you to be and the gifts that operate in your life and we affirm it. Each person knows who they are and what they are called and receives support from the whole body. Unity flows from a shared vision, not forced agreement. We do not have to look the same to move as one. There is unity without uniformity because the kingdom thrives on our diversity.

In our kingdom, wrongdoing does not go unaddressed. It is handled with love and grace with the intent of restoring not punishment. We handle one another with honor never forgetting that we are all Kings and Priest! Remember to be part of the Kingdom of Heaven, you must be a King and Priest. We must never forget, we are surrounded by Kings and we want every King to be treated with honor and supported because we must develop them so that they can establish the Kingdom of Heaven in the territory that their feet touch.

In our kingdom, needs are met! Not just materially, but emotionally, spiritually, and relationally. Remember, when we seek the Kingdom of Heaven first, Jesus promises that all other things will be added to us. We live in a space of overflow, no one lacks, we embody a culture of love and generosity. In our kingdom, God shares His wealth with us and He lays up the wealth of the wicked for those who are righteous (Proverbs 13:22). Those called by His name!

In our kingdoms, we establish generational vision. We do not just live for today. We are preparing other sons "Kings" (male and female) to rule well for tomorrow. We make sure that wisdom is passed to the next generation of Kings. We ensure that the Kingdom of Heaven Legacy is protected, and that faith is multiplied from one generation to the next. We train those who come behind us to walk heavy in their assignment and in the territory that God gives them or prepares for the to take!

CHAPTER 7

BECOMING A PRIEST

But you are a chosen people, a _royal priesthood_ (a kingly or kingdom of priest), a holy nation, God's special possession, that you may declare the praises of him who called you out of darkness into his wonderful light.

— 1 Peter 2:9 NIV

And from Jesus Christ, who is the faithful witness, the firstborn from the dead, and the ruler of the kings of the earth. To him who loves us and has freed us from our sins by his blood and has made us to be a kingdom and _priests_ to serve his God and Father—to him be glory and power for ever and ever! Amen.

— Revelations 1: 5-6

The word "priest" sounds outdated. When we hear it, we tend to picture older men or women dressed in black suits or long robes, wearing white clergy collars — garments that seem rooted in centuries-old traditions. Some people even imagine ceremonial outfits with tall, ornate hats and flowing robes marked by unfamiliar symbols and crosses, all of which may feel disconnected or even confusing in their meaning. But that is not the kind of priest I am – and it is not the kind of priest the scripture is talking about either.

When we hear or see stories about Jesus or read about His journey while in the earth, we never see or hear of Him wearing any of the clothing we see in church. In fact, when they came to apprehend Jesus, Judas had to identify Jesus with a kiss. In Matthew 26:48,

Judas, Jesus' betrayer had given the mob, chief priest, and the elders a sign: "The One I kiss, He's the One; arrest Him." Jesus was dressed like everyone else and looked like his disciples and the people who followed Him. Jesus never adorned himself with religious-based clothing. He is our High Priest, yet he dressed in normal clothing and kept company with those who were part of the Kingdom of God.

Being a priest does not mean we wear special ornamental ceremonial clothing or must look like old people dressed in black suits and robes with clergy collars. This is not the image that Jesus portrayed, and He is a high priest forever (Hebrews 6:20).

Today, a priest is a person who has set their life apart to live holy before God to serve as a mediator between our God and people. Priest pray, provide spiritual guidance, counseling and encouragement, and intercession on behalf of others. When we look at the life of Jesus, we can readily identify all these attributes in His life. He was the greatest example of what our lives should look like as priest. However, there are other attributes of His earthly ministry that should not go unnoticed.

Jesus our high priest – "A Cutting-edge Apostle".

Jesus was a cutting-edge Apostle *"A Sent One"* of God. He came to tear down religious constructs, philosophies, and methodologies and to announce the coming of the Kingdom of God. His teachings bring unity to the church and stand in direct opposition to the religious sects of that day and the denominational structures of today. In that day, it was the Pharisees, Scribes, Essenes, and Sadducees. Today, division shows up in the denominational ministries (i.e. Apostolic, Pentecostal, Baptist, Catholic, Protestant, Christian, etc.). In fact, the root meaning of the word denomination is to divide. The Latin definition of denomination means "a calling by anything other than the proper name." When we choose denominational terms to refer to the Kingdom of God, we are calling the Kingdom of God something that is not proper. Jesus said, the Kingdom of Heaven is at hand (Matthew 3:2). He did not say the Apostolic, Baptist or Pentecostal Kingdom of God is at hand.

The word denomination is nowhere to be found in the Bible. To divide is against the very nature of Jesus Christ and God the Father. There is one Lord, one faith and one baptism, one God and Father of all, who is above all, and through all, and in you all (Ephesians 4:5-6). Jesus constantly reminds us that He and the father are one and He desires for us to be one with them. (John 17:21-23)

Jesus our high priest – "A Rebel in a Robe"

It is important to understand what Jesus came against because, he was not a weak high priest. Some might argue that the bible says that rebellion is as the sin of witchcraft (1Samuel 15:23). That is true when you are rejecting the word of God. Jesus rebelled against demonic powers and constructs that were established in opposition to God by demonic influence in high places (Ephesians 6:12). *Jesus was a rebel in a robe* who was willing to die for what He believe. True players, thugs, rappers, and those who believe in and support free expression should appreciate Jesus's street cred. He was known in the streets for going against those who misrepresented his Father. *Jesus was no joke!* He understands who he was and is. He executed power in natural and spiritual realms.

Jesus is a King from the Kingdom of Heaven who was sent into the earth to establish the Kingdom of God in the earth. He was called a forerunner for a reason. Jesus was a trail blazer who blazed a trail for us to walk through by providing an example of what it looks like to establish God's Kingdom in the earth. More importantly, he is the forerunner for us who has entered the inner sanctuary of God on our behalf and became the high priest forever in the order of Melchizedek.

Jesus had a homeboy edge!

These examples of Jesus as a high priest are proof that Jesus was not just a peaceful, do-gooder. Jesus had a homeboy edge when it came to fighting against things that demonic forces were behind. One day, when Jesus entered the temple courts, He witnessed some people buying and selling animals. This was due to the sacrificial system established by the law of Moses, which was supposed to be a good thing. However, some developed profit-making schemes to rob worshipers who traveled near and far to worship God and offer sacrifices.

Temple inspectors who approved or rejected animals brought by worshipers to sacrifice to God were exploiting the people by untruthful inspections. The inspectors would disapprove of animals brought by worshipers from outside of the temple and force people to buy animals provided by vendors on the inside of the temple. Also, the merchants and money exchanges were exploiting people who came from other countries with high currency exchange rates, often with unfair fees. Jesus seeing this, overturned the tables of the money exchangers and the benches of those selling animals. Then He drove the sellers and money exchangers out of the temple. He said to them, speaking of the temple, "My house will be called a house of prayer, but you are making it a den of robbers" (Matthew 21:13). Jesus was not concerned about who was offended or who was going to try to raise up! He shut that foolishness down.

Jesus was a TRAIL BLAZER who blazed a trail for us to become priest.

According to Revelation 1:5-6, Jesus is the first born from the dead and the ruler of the kings of the earth. Jesus freed us from sin by his blood and made us a kingdom of priest to serve His God and Father. Jesus went first! Making it possible for us to come boldly before the throne of God. Jesus made it possible for us to be a kingdom of priest. So, if we want to be part of the kingdom of heaven, we must be priest!

Jesus was a serious-minded man who came to fulfill God's agenda in the earth and to die for our sins to redeem mankind back to God. Thereby, placing all things under His feet (Ephesians 1:22-23). Understand, no one took His life; He chose to lay down His life for us (John 10:18 No man taketh it from Me, but I lay it down of Myself. I have the power to lay it down, and I have the power to take it again. This commandment have I received from My Father."). It takes a lot of power and strength to be God and subject yourself to being persecuted and killed by those whom you created! Jesus is the true definition of all consuming power bridled by the love of God. He had power to call angels to take care of the light work of killing those who came against Him. Yet, he decided to be nailed to a cross to save mankind.

When they arrested Jesus in the Garden of Gethsemane, Peter drew his sword and cut the servant of those who arrested Him. Jesus rebuked Peter and said:

> "Do you think I cannot call on my Father, and He will all at once put at my disposal more than twelve legions of angels (Matthew 26:53-54)?" Paraphrase: Peter, I need you to understand, they cannot do anything to me, except I allow it!

In Roman military terms, a legion typically consisted of about 6,000 soldiers. So, twelve legions would mean over 72,000 angels. Considering the power attributed to a single angel in biblical accounts (e.g., one angel killed 185,000 Assyrian soldiers in 2 Kings 19:35), this statement emphasized Jesus' immense authority and access to divine power. By making that statement, Jesus demonstrates that His arrest and eventual crucifixion were voluntary. He wasn't powerless; He willingly submitted to God's plan for salvation. This fulfilled prophecies like Isaiah 53, which spoke of the suffering servant who would bear the sins of humanity.

Jesus was and is a powerful high priest with all power in the heavens and the earth! We serve a mighty

God who chose humility because He wants to make us like Him…. Kings and Priest!

Why priest are needed.

Without a priest, no one can approach God. Humanity would not have access to God. In fact, no one can make an offering or give a gift to God without a priest (Hebrews 5:5). When we look at the old testament writings before Moses, offerings could be made directly to God by the people of God. They would build altars and make sacrificial offerings on them. As time progressed, the people of God became so corrupt that the Lord set a tribe called Levi to be priest to serve in the capacity of offering burnt offerings for the sins of the people. These priests would maintain a life that was clean before God so that they could go into the holies of holies and commune with God on behalf of others.

This is not a new idea, God always desired to have a kingdom of priest. We can see God's intention for mankind to be a part of a kingdom of priest dates to the old testament writings. Exodus 19:6, God reminds His people that He brought them out of Egypt carrying them on eagles' wings to Himself. Further, He desires His people to be His treasured possession and if they would fully obey Him and keep His covenant, they would be to Him a kingdom of priest and a holy nation.

God always wanted to be our King! The King of kings. However, Gods people wanted to be like other nations and wanted to have a man as a king. So, God gave them a man name Saul from the tribe of Benjamin to be king. However, the priestly responsibilities and duties remained with those of the tribe of Levi.

You cannot impersonate a priest.

One of the hardest lessons in life is learning not to be full of pride. There are a couple of Kings who made the grave mistake of letting their pride get the best of them causing them to step out of their positions as kings and stepping into the roles that God set aside for priest. Remember, in the Old Testament, priestly duties belonged to the tribe of Levi.

King Saul was about to go into battle against the Philistines in 1 Samuel 13. He was instructed by Samuel the priest and prophet to wait seven days for him to arrive to offer sacrifices and to seek God's favor before the battle. Samuel did not arrive on time; king Saul was impatient and offered the burnt offerings himself. As soon as Saul finished, Samuel arrived and rebuked him, telling him he acted foolishly by not obeying God's command. Offering sacrifices was the role of the priest, not the king. As a result, king Saul lost his kingdom.

King Uzziah reigned for 52 years. He became king at just 16 years old after his father died. He is remembered because initially he was faithful to God. He did what was right in the site of God. He sought God's guidance in everything. He led successful campaigns against his enemies, built advanced machines for war to protect the city, promoted agriculture, dug wells for water and cared for the nation's economy.

King Uzziah's pride got the best of him also. One day he entered the temple and burned incense on the altar. Again, an act reserved for the priest. When confronted by the priest, he would not humble himself. Immediately, leprosy broke out on his skin as a judgement from God. He was quickly removed from the temple and lived the remaining part of his life in isolation.

These kings were not called to be priest. It is very important that we respect God's order and holiness, or we can end up in similar situations. However, we are blessed because Jesus is a high priest after the order of Melchizedek (Hebrews 5:6) and has made us kings and priest. Bringing the office of king and priest together in one. We can go before God without needing someone to go for us.

The order of Melchizedek combines King and Priest

Melchizedek means "king of righteousness"; also, "king of Salem" means "king of peace." Without father or mother, without genealogy, without beginning of days or end of life, resembling the Son of God, he remains a priest forever. ...

Then Melchizedek king of Salem brought out bread and wine. He was priest of God Most High, and he blessed Abram, saying, "Blessed be Abram by God Most High, Creator of heaven and earth. Genesis 14:18-19 NIV

Bread and wine are the trademark of Melchizedek ministry. We saw this same display at the last supper.

Jesus gave to his disciple's bread and wine indicating to them that the priesthood of Melchizedek has been restored in Him. Transitioning out of the order (law) of Moses back to the order of Melchizedek which is the original eternal order of priesthood where KINGSHIP and PRIESTHOOD are combined. So, we are a kingdom of KINGS and PRIEST belonging to the order of Melchizedek not Levi. We are in the priesthood of Melchizedek like Jesus. We follow the path of Jesus as our King and High Priest.

Where our forerunner, Jesus, has entered on our behalf. He has become a high priest forever, in the order of Melchizedek. Hebrews 6:20

In the past, when the priest died, they were dead and could not continue in the office of the priest. Their priesthood ended with their death. Now in Jesus we have a High Priest who lives forever. In this regard, Jesus is likened to Melchizedek. Melchizedek did not have a mother or a father. He had no beginning or ending of days. He simply is. His life never ends.

Without father, without mother and without descent, having neither beginning of days nor end of life, but made like unto the Son of God, he abides a priest continually. Hebrews 7:3

Jesus lives forever; His priesthood is permanent! He can save us completely when we go to God through Him because He always lives to intercede for us. Hebrews 7:23-25 says it best:

Now there have been many of those priests, since death prevented them from continuing in office; but because Jesus lives forever, he has a permanent priesthood. Therefore, he can save completely those who come to God through him, because he always lives to intercede for them. Hebrews 7:23-25

Priest after the order of Melchizedek Means What!

Melchizedek was a king priest! The king of Salem (peace) and a priest. Melchizedek has no beginning or ending of days. He did not have a father or mother. Making his kingship and priesthood forever. Therefore, Jesus is a king and priest forever. Making us kings and priest as the sons of God forever. Hence the term King of kings and Lord of lords.

And from Jesus Christ, who is the faithful witness, the firstborn from the dead, and the ruler of the kings of the earth. To him who loves us and has freed us from our sins by his blood and has made us to be a kingdom and priests to serve his God and Father—to him be glory and power forever and ever! Amen. Revelations 1: 5-6

Our Priestly Duties.

Hebrews 13:15-16 (NKJV) Therefore by Him let us continually offer the sacrifice of praise to God, that is, the fruit of our lips, giving thanks to His name. But do not forget to do good and to share, for with such sacrifices God is well pleased.

As priest, we offer four sacrifices: The *Sacrifice of Praise*, *Thanksgiving*, *Doing Good* and *Sharing with Others*. These sacrifices can be grouped into two areas. Our Praise which is vertical and Goodness which is horizontal.

> Vertical - Praise. We thank Jesus with the fruit of our lips through worship, prayer, and gratitude.

> Horizontal - Goodness. We express our thanks to God for what He has done in our lives by how we treat others through our kindness, generosity, and service.

Jesus said, in Matthew 22:37–40:

> Love the Lord your God with all your heart and with all your soul and with all your mind. This is the first and greatest commandment. And the second is like it: Love your neighbor as yourself. All the Law and the Prophets hang on these two commandments.

Priest offers their lives as a sacrifice to God.

Apostle Paul tells the church in Romans 12:1-2 that they should offer their bodies as a living sacrifice and live a life that is holy and pleasing to God. In the eyes of Apostle Paul, a holy life is a true and proper expression of our worship to God. Further, Apostle Paul explains that we should not pattern our lives after those in the world. He suggests that we should, rather be transformed by changing and renovating our minds to align with the will of God. Then we should be positioned to understand how to please God.

Holiness is not a popular stance to take now days. A standard of holy and pure living seems to have faded. Some people want to straddle the fence having one foot in God and the other in the world system. Making it difficult to determine if they are saved or not. Another term for this is "mixture". Mixture is diluted devotion to God. When our sacrifice or worship becomes compromised, corrupt or impure and unacceptable to God. The Lord told the church at Laodicea," I wish you were hot or cold, but you are neither one or the other! So, because you are lukewarm—neither hot nor cold, I am about to spit you out of my mouth." We must make a choice to be completely given to a life of sacrifice if as priest we are to offer acceptable sacrifices to God. Revelations 3:15

Priest offers the sacrifice of praise to God.

Therefore, by Him let us continually offer the sacrifice of praise to God, that is, the *fruit of our lips*, giving thanks to His name. But do not forget to do good and to share, for with such sacrifices God is well pleased (Hebrews 13:15-16). The fruit of our lips refers to the words, praise, and thanksgiving that we speak from our mouths when they're directed toward honoring, glorifying, and giving thanks to God. This is a metaphor that shows us just as trees bear fruit, our praise is fruit that our mouths bear.

The bible says that from the abundance of the heart the mouth speaks. Interestingly, the words of praise and worship come from the overflow of our heart. Abundance means more than what we need.

It must not be easy for us as mankind to release praise and worship to God from a place of abundance. Because Apostle Paul would not have referred to it as a sacrifice. To sacrifice, means to give up something valuable in selfless devotion to God. Our praise cost us something because no matter how we feel nor what is going on in our lives, we need to tap into a place in our heart that is more than what we need to offer up worship and praise because of who He is.

When we hear the word heart in the Bible, it is referring to the brain. Before we go into praise and worship, we must prepare our minds to offer worship to God that cost us something. So, if we are going to offer a sacrifice, we must pay that ahead of the time of worship. We must provide our minds with "abundance of thought". Meaning we must take time to meditate on how blessed we are and how wonderful God is. Making sure that we spend time having inner dialogue and reflection on God and the things of God. An "abundance of thought" filled with rich reflection, intentional focus and intellectual overflow. It is our desire that when we fill our minds with "abundance of thought", it will shape the *"fruit of our lips"* to be released to God.

God does not want drive-by worship that is the equivalent of a one-night stand. God wants to be on our minds daily before we come into a space of worship with Him. He wants to know us for more than a couple of hours before we get intimate with Him. Quality time in prayer, meditation and thought creates an abundant space of understanding about God for us to base our praise and adoration on. The Apostle Paul said it best, "that I might know Him in the fellowship of His suffering and in the power of His resurrection. (Philippians 3:10-12) An "abundance of thought" creates knowledge and understanding into who God really is and is the foundation of our intimacy with God.

As Priest we offer thanksgiving to His name!

We offer expressions of gratitude in Jesus's name because Jesus' sacrifice has given us access to the presence of God. Our expression is more than the words that proceed from our mouths, it is a heart, mind, and lifestyle that is postured in a place of gratitude. That causes us to make declarations about who He is and what He has done for us.

We profess His name openly in reverence with deep honor and respect (Hebrews 13:15). We say His name honorably in prayer thanking Him for saving us, loving us, and walking with us. We speak His name in gratitude in conversation giving Him credit for our strength and blessings. We speak His name out loud in adoration in our worship as we speak directly to Him as the one who is the author and finisher of our faith and belief. We thank Him by name "Jesus our Redeemer", "Jesus our Peace", and Jesus our Provider". We lift our voices, and our hearts in thanksgiving because He is faithful. "Enter His gates with thanksgiving and His courts with praise; give thanks to Him and praise His name." (Psalm 100:4).

As we reflect on Jesus, we offer thanksgiving to His name because of how great He is, we share our testimony to others of how He saved, healed and transformed us. We share our testimonies with our children, friends, coworkers, and the world. (1 Chronicles 16:8) Thanking God in every season. We thank Him in joy because of His goodness and mercy, in struggle because of His presence and promise, and in uncertainty because He is faithful and unchanging.

As Priest we do Good to Others!

We must be mindful that as priest, we are His workmanship, created in Christ Jesus for good works, which God prepared beforehand that we should walk in them. (Ephesians 2:10) Our worship and thanksgiving are not about what we say only. It's also about what we do! We are not accidents; we are intentionally crafted and designed by God Himself for good works.

It might be hard to see yourself as someone designed for good works because of past pains or past performance. When people hurt us, sometimes we evolve from those situations and hurt others. We created memories that don't want to let go of us. In these situations, it can be hard to forgive ourselves and others. What we must do is grab hold to the idea that Jesus made us priest and we are in Him now and we have new DNA. Our genetic code has been changed. The molecules that carry our genetic code have been changed. The blueprint for who we are and the instructions by which we have been made have been revised. The Bible says that if any man be in Christ he is a new creature: old things are passed away; behold, all things are become new. (2 Corinthians 5:17)

As priest, God equipes us unto good works. Not according only to our standards but to a better standard based on what is right but what is righteous. Righteous works! Actions that are right based on God's judgement. Rooted in our faith and commitment to God and our purpose in Him. Actions that we make from a place of worship. Worship that comes from an "abundance of thought" and thanksgiving that produce sacrificial acts of kindness, love, and service that are made as unto God that benefit others.

As Priest we do Share with Others!

When we share, we reveal the generosity of God. It is more than charity, it is ministry. Sharing is part of our service, our calling, lifestyle, and overflow of who we are in Christ. Sharing is an act of love. Apostle John asks the question in 1 John 3:17, how can the love of God be in a person who has material possessions and sees a brother or sister in need but has no pity on them.

Sharing builds unity. We see this in Acts 2:44-45 when all the believers were together and had everything in common, they sold property and possessions to give to anyone who had need. It is important that as priest we understand that sharing and giving to others is equivalent to sowing seed into the ground. You cannot expect to harvest something that you did not plant in the ground. The principle of "seedtime and harvest" is simple. You cannot expect to have a positive outcome or blessing represented by *harvest* if you have not taken the time to *plant seeds* by investing actions and efforts into someone else. Genesis 8:22 As long as the earth endures, seedtime and harvest will never cease. Whatever you seed you plant (share or give), in its proper season (time) will produce a harvest (return on your labor).

When we share our resources in the form of money, food, and shelter. Share our time by listening, helping, and serving. Giving encouragement, wisdom, and truth through our words spoken in love. Sharing miracles and the blessings of God by releasing our faith through our testimony, prayer, and the Gospel. We show how deeply we love, worship, and know God. A love that is more than words or speech but with actions and truth. (1 John 3:18)

Blessings in Fulfilling our Priestly Duties

When we offer these sacrifices as priest, the Bible says with such sacrifices God is well pleased. When God accepts our sacrifices, He responds to our heart. James 4:8 says draw near to God, and He will draw near to you. When we offer a sacrifice from a pure heart filled with love and gratitude, God shows up! Understand, we can never earn God's presence. However, our offering becomes an invitation for intimacy with God.

Abel's sacrifice pleased God because it was from his first and best. (Genesis 4:4) God honored Abel with His attention and favor. Abel's sacrifice caused God to look on him and his sacrifice with favor. When favor is released, doors are opened or closed, needs are met, resources are multiplied, and people are blessed through you.

When you sacrifice, God multiplies what you give. Luke 6:38 states: Give, and it will be given to you… for with the measure you use, it will be measured to you. When your sacrifice pleases God, He receives it and multiplies it! Your needs do not go unmet. Sometimes, God impresses it upon us to give more when we feel like we have little to nothing to offer. When we step out in faith and give our last word of encouragement, prayer in belief that God is going to move, financial resources to help someone settle a debt, or time when we are exhausted and want to rest, God gives a manifold blessing back to us that we don't have room to receive.

Understand, God sees and rewards. God is just; he will not forget your work and the love you have shown him as you have helped his people and continue to help them. (Hebrews 6:10, NIV) God watched you cry tears in secret, He witness every act of kindness and obedience, and He remembers and rewards! When God is pleased, He trust you with more! More revelation! More responsibility! More influence! Then He allows you to step into a greater assignment! *"Well done, good and faithful servant... You have been faithful with a few things; I will put you in charge of many things."* (Matthew 25:23)

We are priest!

We offer sacrifices and intercession in heavenly places in Christ! We are those who really rule the world for God because we learn to minister as Priest and rule as Kings because we are heirs to an everlasting throne in Christ!

CONCLUSION

The Call Still Stands!

Congratulations, you've made it to the end of this book—but you're only at the beginning of your journey.

This isn't just about manhood. It's about divine identity. About choosing to become the man heaven recognizes, hell fears, and the world desperately needs. A man who walks in sonship—anchored in the Father's love. A man who reigns with kingdom authority—as a king, not a pawn. A man who ministers in the trenches of everyday life with the compassion and boldness of a priest. This isn't the costume we wear. It's a mantle we carry.

This world has enough men chasing titles, status, and validation. But God is raising up sons—healed, whole, and humble. He's anointing kings—not for thrones of ego, but for tables of justice, provision, and influence. He's calling priests—not for pulpits alone, but for purpose-filled presence in every sphere.

You are becoming that man.

So, stand firm. Stay rooted. Keep becoming. Don't go back to what you were before. You're not just *any* man—you are *His* man.

The call to sonship, kingship, and priesthood is not a suggestion—it's a commissioning. Step into it with fire in your heart, truth in your mouth, and purpose in your stride.

BECOMING A MAN, SON, KING & PREIST TODAY!

Because when you know who you are, you'll stop chasing what you're not.

ABOUT THE AUTHOR

Willie G. Miller Jr. isn't just a preacher—he's a problem for hell. A bold voice in this generation, Will is an author, mentor, and apostolic leader called to activate identity, uproot generational strongholds, and raise up men who walk in power, purity, and purpose. He's not interested in cute church culture or soft sermons— he's building Kingdom assassins with fire in their bones and deliverance in their mouths.

Through his teaching, writing, and mentorship, Will equips young men to confront inner chaos, break toxic patterns, and embrace their role as sons, kings, and priests. With a background in ministry, leadership development, and prophetic instruction, he fuses real-life grit with deep biblical revelation to spark true transformation.

Whether he's mentoring one-on-one, preaching with fire, or launching disruptive Kingdom-based resources, Will's mission is clear: Wake up King-Priest. Build legacies that scare the devil. He currently leads a movement of emerging Kingdom men across digital platforms and in-person gatherings under the mantle of spiritual formation and generational restoration.

Will is the senior leader along with his wife of Impact Global Ministries located in District Heights Maryland. He is the founder of WillieMillerMinistries.com—a hub for books, mentorship programs, devotionals, prophetic training, and raw truth that pushes people out of cycles and into destiny.

CONNECT AND SHARE

If you enjoyed reading Becoming a Man, Son, King & Priest Today! Please purchase copies for others who can benefit and leave or send a review on the website where you purchased this book.

Connect with the author online:

    Facebook: Willie Miller
                Impact Global Ministries

    Instagram: Willie Miller.3150

    Websites: WillieMillerMinistries.com
                ImpactGlobalMinistries.org

REFERENCES

Chapter 1: Becoming A Man

1. Coming of Age. (2018). *Bar/Bat Mitzvah, Jewish Museum London.* Retrieved from: https://www.youtube.com/watch?v=dl2EgHMU5G4&t=90s
2. EBS World. (2023). *A Boy's Coming of Age, The Hamar of Ethiopia, Part 1 Exploring the Origin of Humanity* [Video]. YouTube: https://www.youtube.com/watch?v=GCLbMN5RD3Q
3. Covey, Steven. (2013). *7 Habits of Highly Effective People.* Simon & Schuster.
4. Lutz, C. (2014). *Holy Spirit.* Retrieved from: https://fragrancearise.com/2014/08/21/holy-spirit/

Chapter 2: How and Where to Think

1. Remez, S. (n.d.). *Mind Power – The Power of Thoughts.* Retrieved from: https://www.successconsciousness.com/blog/concentration-mind-power/mind-power/
2. The United Negro College Fund. Retrieved from: https://uncf.org/about
3. Murphy, J. (1963). *How to Unleash the Power of Your Subconscious Mind.* Penguin Random House and JMW Group.
4. Allen, J. (1951). *As a Man Thinketh.* Mount Vernon, N.Y.: Peter Pauper Press.

Chapter 3: Getting an Understanding

1. Herold, Cameron. (2018). *Vivid Vision: A Remarkable Tool for Aligning Your Business Around a Shared Vision of the Future.* Lioncrest Publishing

Chapter 4: How to Speak

1. Baquet, Dean (2018). *Jay-Z and Dean Baquet, in Conversation.* New York Times. Time mark: 25:40. Retrieved from: https://www.youtube.com/watch?v=XbuQAbG2AZ0

Chapter 5: Becoming a Son

1. Early, Tim. (unpublished). *Apostolic Fatherhood and Sonship – Relational Kingdom Ministry.* Unpublished White Paper.
2. Powers, Christi (2013). *Three Gifts.* Going Beyond the Familiar. Retrieved December 2024 from: http://www.goingbeyondthefamiliar.com/2013/12/three-gifts.html

Chapter 6: Becoming a King

1. Monroe, Myles (2017). *The Characteristics of a King Part 1.* Monroe Global. Time mark: 4:30. Retrieved from: https://www.youtube.com/watch?v=Vn-K840Fllg&t=5s
2. Allers, R., & Minkoff, R. (1994). The Lion King. Buena Vista Pictures.
3. Monroe, Myles (2018). *The Characteristics of a King Part 2.* Monroe Global. Time mark: 1:26:44. Retrieved from: https://www.youtube.com/watch?v=N-gvD6fOyC8

Chapter 7: Becoming a Priest

None